If I Can...

TIMELESS VALUES FOR TODAY

Inspired by the poem
IF by Rudyard Kipling
&
The Bhagavad Gita

Compiled by
Paul Palmarozza
Jerome Toole

Published in India by
Dr. Hari Prasad Kanoria
on behalf of Contempory News
3 Middle Road, Hastings,
Kolkata - 700002, India

"You have the privilege to do anything for the world. In helping the world we really help ourselves"

Dr. H.P. Kanoria
Chairman
Srei foundation

If I Can... Timeless Values for Today

If I Can has brought together two very important influences in this person's life: the poem IF by Rudyard Kipling and the study of Philosophy, especially the BHAGAVAD GITA, one of the most beloved and respected scriptures of the Indian spiritual tradition.* The idea behind the project arose in response to a perceived need for people, especially younger people, to be reminded of moral values and virtues in a form appropriate for today. The hope is that when reminded of these universal values and how they are natural to everyone, people will be inspired to try and live them, i.e. make the words come alive.

IF

The poem IF, a copy of which was given to me by my cousin when I was 17 years old, describes the virtues and values that one needs to follow to attain the fullness of manhood. It made an immediate impression and I hung it up in my room as a continual reminder.
Some of the verses were so powerful that they have stuck with me throughout my life:

- If you can keep your head when all about you
  Are losing theirs, and blaming it on you,

- If you can meet with triumph and disaster,
  And treat those two imposters just the same.

- If you can fill the unforgiving minute
  With sixty seconds worth of distance run...

Note: The well-known Indian historian and writer Khushwant Singh asserts that Rudyard Kipling's famous poem IF is "the essence of the message of The Bhagavad Gita in English."

What was so valuable to me as a young person was the challenge inherent in the question If you can... The final lines of the poem provided the incentive for trying hard to meet the challenge fully.

If you can... Then

*Yours is the Earth and everything that is in it,
And...which is more...you'll be a Man, my Son!*

My understanding of what it means to 'be a Man' has now transformed to mean living up to our full potential as human beings-male or female - to realise our true Self, and to be able to answer fully the universal question 'Who am I' ?

Philosophy/The Bhagavad Gita
Later in life I took up the study of Philosophy and read works from several different traditions, from East and West. Of the great scriptures, the one

that has made the most lasting impression is the BHAGAVAD GITA. Over a 20-year period I wrote out the 700 verses, using a calligraphic script for the English and the devanagari script for the Sanskrit and taking time along the way to consider the meaning of the key words in each verse.

Truly a labour of love.

Recently while studying the GITA, as it is called, with a small group of friends, we reached chapter 16, where Lord Krishna gives to Arjuna a description of 27 divine qualities of a human being. These qualities or virtues are natural to man and are easily recognised, even if they are not made manifest in daily life. They set out a model, much like IF, but in far greater detail.

Some of the virtues included in the text are:
- Fearlessness/Courage
- Selflessness
- Charity
- Self-Control
- Harmlessness/non-violence
- Truthfulness
- Absence of Anger

Seeing a Need

What prompted the next step on the journey of this project was the observation of the challenging conditions facing young people today. While problems at the material level, which are by no means the same in developed Western cultures as in the developing countries of Asia and Africa, have drawn a great deal of media attention, there has not been sufficient acknowledgement of a more fundamental issue- the need for sound spiritual education and guidance.

The rich, famous and powerful people in Western society seem to be setting the agenda for life's values, focusing on pleasure as the way to happiness. The problems which have arisen as a result are actually due to excess- exceeding the reasonable limits. It is now generally accepted that our society indulges in too much food, drink, drugs, activity and sensual pleasure for our own long-term welfare. The right measure, i.e. knowing what is enough, when to stop, has been lost and we are finding that it is difficult to change our established patterns. As a result the key values in our materialistic, consumer- based society have become Wealth, Fame, Power and Pleasure, instead of the virtues and values advocated by all the great teachers.

What is happening in the West is being watched carefully by the web & mobile savvy younger generations of the East. The real danger is that they may choose to ignore their respective spiritual traditions and instead rush to imitate our mistaken measures of success.

For many idealistic young people there is a real awareness that these materialistic values of society are not the right way. For them the danger is that their frustration with the greed and excess in society can all too easily turn to anger, violence, crime or bored resignation.

The net impact of this is that many of the current generation who have not seen enough examples of virtue in action have inevitably come more under the influence of the popular media in establishing their values of life.

Spiritual Guidance

When we look more closely into what the various religious, philosophical and spiritual traditions have to say about virtue, we find a common message: Virtue is natural to a human being and is the greatest source of true happiness.

The great teachers of mankind - Socrates/Plato, Confucius, Mahavira, Buddha, Lao Tzu, Krishna, Jesus Christ and the Prophets of the Bible, to name a few, - all offered virtue as the moral compass to guide our life towards greater happiness and the full realisation of our potential.

For an individual who is able to live these virtues and values there is finer discrimination and judgement in all aspects of life. The material world is enjoyed, but in the right measure and at the right time. Such a person also develops a greater degree of self-confidence and is able to make the right decisions, unaffected by popular opinion.

As the desire for happiness is universal, the question arises as to why it is not accessed? Why aren't we all more virtuous in our thoughts, words and actions?

The answer seems to be that our inherent knowledge and awareness are covered over by the clouds of ignorance -an ignoring of what is our true heritage. We need to be continually reminded of the better way forward.

The Next Step on The Journey

What came to mind when reading the verses in the GITA was to present these 27 virtues in a form that young people can relate to as they try to cope with a very uncertain world.

It seemed that the structure and phrasing of IF might be a useful start, so I took a step into the dark and wrote verses for each of the 27 divine qualities, starting each with If you can and then continuing in the same metre as used by Kipling. The aim was to highlight one aspect or example of that virtue/ quality. With no training in poetry I sought and received some help from my daughter Jessica who is reading English at Oxford and has a great love of language. Here are some examples of what emerged:

- FEARLESSNESS/COURAGE
  If you can to the howling mob close your ears
  Yet stand and stay to fight when you are right;
  If you can take one step forward to your fears
  Sending their darkened images to flight...

- CHARITY / WORK FOR OTHERS
  If you can change the words of the wise to deeds
  And let fine virtue be your living guide;
  If you can seek to meet your neighbour's needs
  And not what you want to have on your side...

- AUSTERITY / SELF - DISCIPLINE
  If you can resist passion's strong, subtle pull
  And follow only the moderate way;
  If you can read the signs which say you are full
  And thus know when to stop and when to stay...

- ABSENCE OF ANGER
  If you can master all your wild emotions,
  Arising from frustration of desire;
  If you can bring to calm all the commotion s
  And let hot anger's fiery flames retire...

- SERENITY / CONTENTMENT
  If you can curb the waste of precious power
  Not seeking the approval of other;
  Resting content like a beautiful flower
  Neither less nor greater than another...

Feedback & A New Direction

When I showed this poetic offering to a few people, a positive response was received about the idea and some very useful suggestions were offered aimed at making it more relevant to young people:

- Make it IF I CAN... instead of IF YOU CAN...
  The reason given is that it would have a more powerful impact for younger people if the statement was in the form of an acknowledgement by the individual, a self-affirmation, of the value of the direction offered by the statement and of the need for self- effort; i.e. If I can; as compared to listening to the guidance of another telling me what I should do, i.e. If you can.

- Develop an APP
  Make the material available on phones, tablets and the web. Encourage people to share their views with others via the social media sites such as Facebook and Twitter.

- Use quotes about these values from the various spiritual teachers and traditions

From some others the advice was that the subject is one that needs to be brought to the attention of older people as well, so books, printed versions and E-books, should also be used as vehicles for communicating the message. I agreed with the suggestions and...

SO...

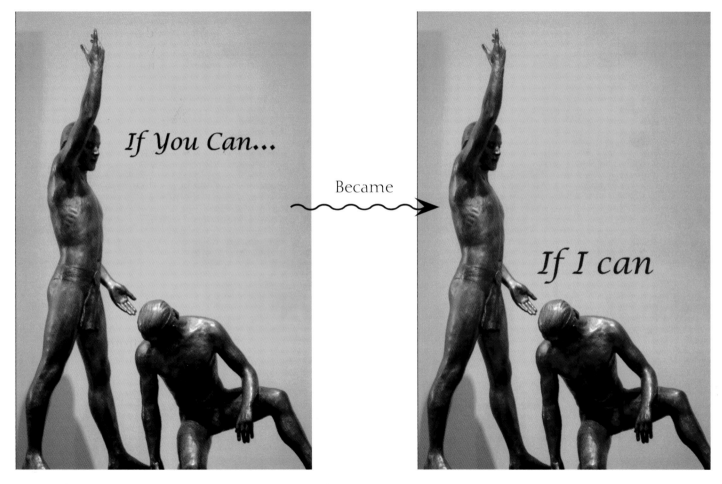

Became

The 'If I Can' App

The App emerged in the form of a daily If I can statement about a virtue/value/fine quality from a list of 73, divided into 10 main themes:

- LOVE
  (Benevolence, Charity, Compassion, Sacrifice, Forgiveness, Absence of Hatred)

- SELFLESSNESS
  (Humility, Kindness, Gentleness, Courtesy, Gratitude, Generosity)

- COURAGE
  (Fearlessness, Determination, Steadfastness, Perseverance, Strength, Enthusiasm)

- HARMLESSNESS
  (Self-Control, Obedience, Patience, Tolerance, Absence of Criticism, Absence of Anger)

- JUSTICE
  (Lawfulness, Mercy, Loyalty, Respect, Duty, Service)

- TEMPERANCE
  (Moderation, Prudence, Harmony, Tactfulness, Dignity, Absence of Greed)

- TRUTHFULLNESS
  (Trust, Honour, Integrity, Reliability, Sincerity, Friendship)

- WISDOM
  (Detachment, Discrimination, Consistency, Purity of Mind, Righteousness, Meditation)

- BEING PRESENT
  (Equanimity, Serenity, Stillness, Simplicity, Creativity, Consciousness)

- SPIRITUALITY
  (Devotion, Faith, Hope, Peace, Unity, Freedom, Beauty, Happiness, Liberation)

Over the period of a year there are 5 statements about each virtue (5 x 73 = 365). To enhance the impact of each statement the following features are included:

- The statement, written in a fine script, is superimposed on an image. The image- a photo, illustration or work of art- may relate directly to the content of the statement or it may just be a beautiful picture designed to arrest the attention of the observer.

- A 2nd page, accessed by touching/clicking on the image. This offers a quote from various spiritual, philosophical, and inspirational sources, relating to the particular virtue highlighted that day.

- Item 73 , which is repeated 5 times in the year, is a Then statement, one which speaks of the consequences of fulfilling the If I can challenge. They are like the final statement of IF :

Yours is the Earth and everything that is in it, And...which is more...you'll be a Man, my Son!

Here is an example:

Delivery Media

Experience has shown that efforts can be helped through the power of a group of like-minded people working together in a common way towards a common aim. The social media revolution, while not the full answer, is nevertheless an instrument for our time to help bring about a greater sense of sharing.

In order to reach as many people as possible the material is made available in several formats:

- As a mobile App available in the Apple and other App stores
- In a format suitable for an I-pad or similar tablet device
- Online via a special website which automatically sends out a daily email to its subscribers who can access the App via a phone, tablet and/or a computer
- As a book, in print and e-book formats

The Project Team

This endeavour has been a multi-generational development project. While the idea for the project has come from someone having just entered his 8th decade, the main development work has been undertaken by two young people; Jerome Toole- Project Manager and Sanjay Poyzer-App Developer, each around 20 years old.

The contributions of photos and text have also come from a mixed group of senior experienced people along with some very talented young men and women.

Funding

The project began as a self-funded initiative with the main costs being the hourly rate paid to the two key players. As it became clear that substantially more funding would be required to make the vision a reality, a propitious meeting occurred with trustees of a charity, The Leon MacLaren Art Trust. This registered charity, named after the founder of the School of Economic Science, has as its focus 'to educate the public in such arts, music or literature as in the opinion of the trustees shall convey knowledge of any appreciation of the moral, spiritual and cultural traditions of humanity'.

The proposal for funding to complete the development of the If I Can App was approved by them, thus making possible its launch in 2013. Through another very propitious meeting at a Technology exhibition held in London we met Aress, an Indian-based organisation who specialises in App development. When they heard our story, noting that it was to be a charitable offering, the CEO, Mr Rahul Malhotra offered to help us with the development at no charge, as their charitable offering. This is a VERY generous offer as their knowledge and skills will enable the project team to more effectively deal with the daunting technical challenges.

In order to enable as many people as possible to access the App there will be no charge. Users will be given the option to offer a financial donation. Any funds in excess of that needed to upgrade and maintain the system will be offered to charities, including our benefactor, The Leon MacLaren Art Trust.

Users will also be offered the option to contribute images, their own ''If I Can' statement and relevant quotes. In this way the subsequent versions of the App will be based on the knowledge and experience of the community.

Summary

We believe the If I Can project,, which includes this book can, make a contribution in helping individuals change their self-image by reminding them of their true nature. Recognition of this would lead naturally to greater confidence, a finer awareness of the moral principles of life and a more positive attitude towards service for the benefit of others.

The project will continue to be an adventure, a journey into the unknown. Our modus operandi will be to remain in the present moment and from a point of stillness and balance make each decision, one step at a time. As the Buddha said to one of his disciples on how matters progress naturally:

Drop

by

drop,

the

water

pot

is

filled.

To find out how you can access the App please go to the website- www.ificanapp.com.

Finally, sincere thanks to Nick Downs for his tireless work in designing this book and to Dr Hari Prasad Kanoria for publishing it.

I have found the paradox, that if you love until it hurts, there can be no more hurt, only more love.

Mother Teresa

LOVE

If I can keep
my face towards

Love's sunshine

and not let the
shadows of hate
mess up my mind...

Please bless us with benevolence and keep us away from miserliness.

Rig Veda

BENEVOLENCE

If I can see
that a benevolent
person is like a fountain
nourishing the earth...

Charity and devotion differ no more, the one from the other, than the flame and the fire.

St Francis de Sales

CHARITY

If I can observe
that when there is
charity & wisdom,
there is beauty &
happiness...

Teach this triple truth to all:
a generous heart, kind speech, and a
life of service and compassion are
the things which renew humanity.

Buddha

COMPASSION

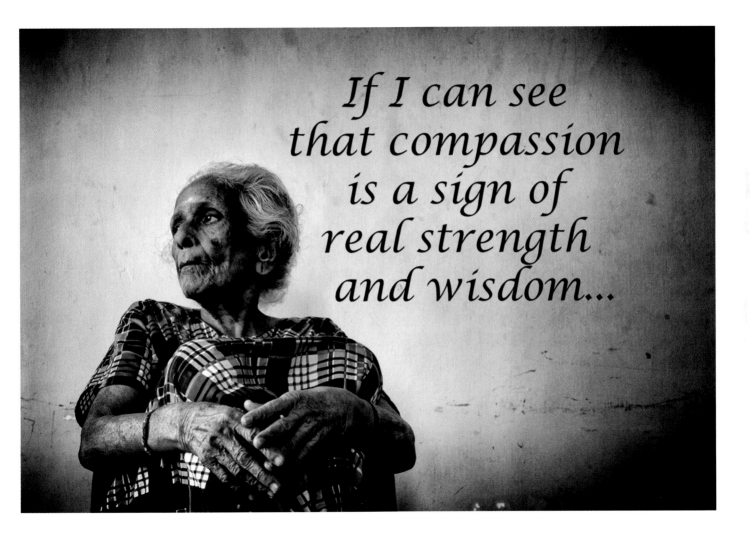

The sacrifice which causes sorrow to the doer of the sacrifice is no sacrifice. Real sacrifice lightens the mind of the doer and gives him a sense of peace and joy.

Mahatma Gandhi

SACRIFICE

If I can ask each day

what I can do for others
rather than what they
can do for me...

Let us forgive each other - only then will we live in peace.

Tolstoy

FORGIVENESS

If I can subdue my anger by gentle thoughts of forgiveness...

Shall I not inform you
of a better act than
fasting, alms, and prayers?
Making peace between one another:
enmity and malice
tear up heavenly rewards by the roots.

Muhammad

ABSENCE OF HATRED

If I can avoid reacting to the arguments of the arrogant...

Only a life lived for others is worth living.

Einstein

SELFLESSNESS

If I can see the
error in calling
everything about me

THIS

and everything
about others,

THAT

Do you desire to construct a vast and lofty fabric? Think first about the foundations of humility. The higher your structure is to be, the deeper must be its foundation.

St Augustine

HUMILITY

If I can ignore the
hollow echoes of applause

and so calm
the heart,
beating
fast for fame...

*Kindness in words
creates confidence.
Kindness in thinking
creates profoundness.
Kindness in giving
creates love.*

Lao Tzu

KINDNESS

If I can

know that

kindness

given
or
received,

opens

the heart...

Gentleness can only be expected from the strong.

Leo Buscaglia

GENTLENESS

If I can see that nothing is as strong as gentleness

and nothing as gentle as real strength...

There is a courtesy of the heart; it is allied to love. From it springs the purest courtesy in the outward behaviour.

Goethe

COURTESY

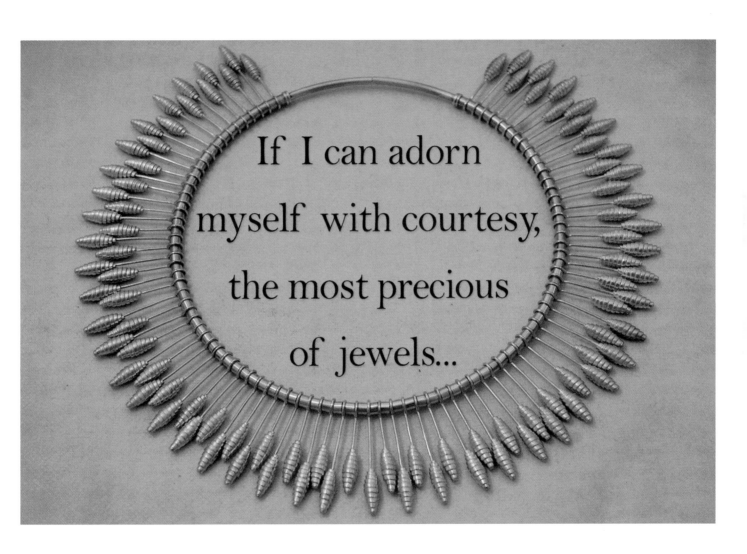

If I can adorn myself with courtesy, the most precious of jewels...

No one who achieves success does so without acknowledging the help of others. The wise and confident acknowledge this help with gratitude.

Alfred North Whitehead

GRATITUDE

It is more blessed to give than to receive.

Jesus

GENEROSITY

If I can give
without any
thought of
getting
something
in return...

He who keeps his head high and courage in his heart, he sets in motion those fine still powers, which make every step through life easier for him.

Ralph Waldo Trine

COURAGE

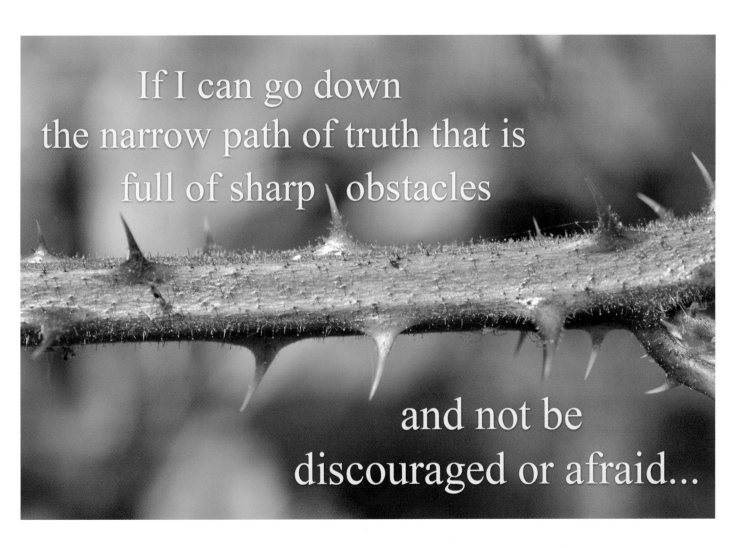

If I can go down
the narrow path of truth that is
full of sharp obstacles

and not be
discouraged or afraid...

You gain strength, courage, and confidence by every experience in which you really stop to look fear in the face.

Eleanor Roosevelt

FEARLESSNESS

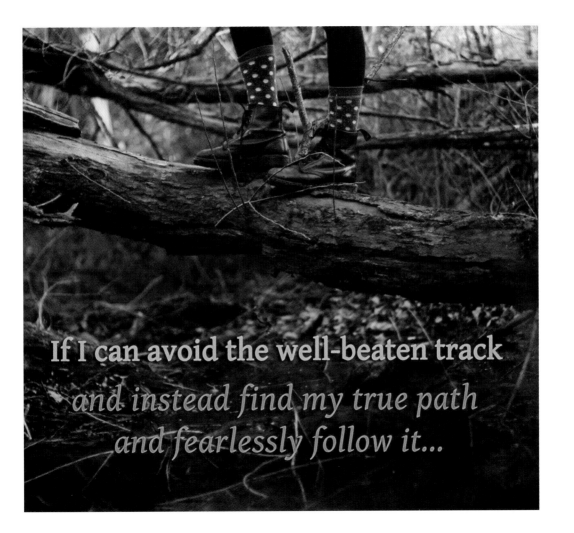

If I can avoid the well-beaten track
and instead find my true path
and fearlessly follow it...

Never, never, never, never give up.

Winston Churchill

DETERMINATION

When you have seen your aim,

hold to it,

firm and unshakeable.

Dhammapada

STEADFASTNESSS

IF I CAN HOLD FIRM, BE STEADFAST AND RESOLVED AND WAIT FOR THE RIGHT MOMENT   TO ACT...

Perseverance is a sign of will power. He who stays where he is, endures.

Lao Tzu

PERSEVERANCE

If I can learn to hold on
even tighter
when things get tough...

When you have faith, you have energy.

Thich Nhat Hanh

STRENGTH/ENERGY

If I can overcome the
urge to put off
till tomorrow
that which needs
doing today...

Enthusiasm
is the mother of effort,
and without it
nothing great
was ever achieved.

Ralph Waldo Emerson

ENTHUSIASM

If I can develop that

inner feeling & belief

that anything is possible...

Non-violence is not a cloistered virtue to be practised by the individual for peace and final salvation, it is a rule for society. It is the greatest force at the disposal of mankind.

Mahatma Gandhi

HARMLESSNESS

If I can avoid doing any harm;

physical, mental or emotional,

to any other being...

Should not all men hold self-control to be the foundation of all virtue and first establish this firmly in their souls?

Plato

SELF-CONTROL

If you do not wish to be prone to anger, do not feed the habit; give it nothing which may tend to its increase.

Epictetus

ABSENCE OF ANGER

If I can remember that my anger harms me more than the person who is the object of my anger...

He who obeys with
modesty will be worthy
some day of being
allowed to command.

Cicero

OBEDIENCE

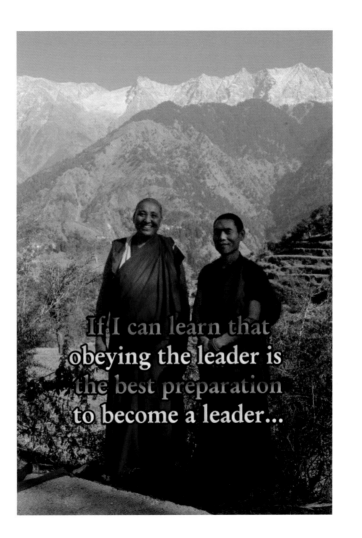

If I can learn that
obeying the leader is
the best preparation
to become a leader...

If you do not cover yourself on every side with the shield of patience, you will not long remain without wounds.

Thomas a` Kempis

PATIENCE

People were created for
the sake of one another.
Either teach them
or bear with them.

Marcus Aurelius

TOLERANCE

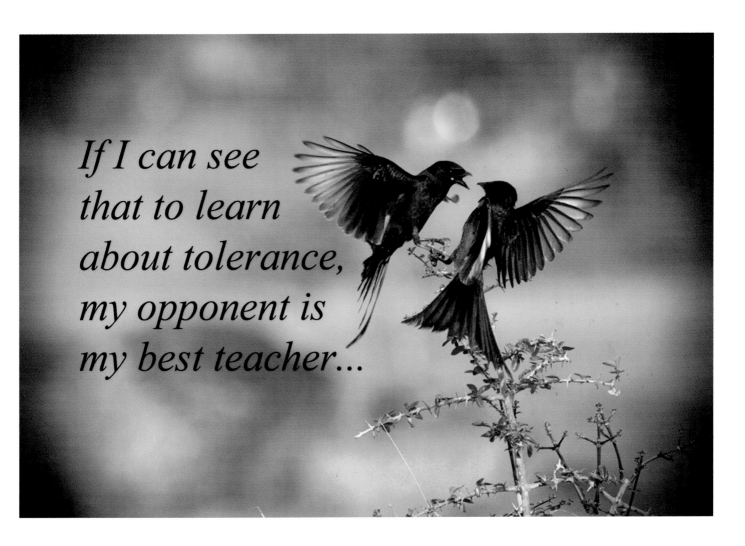

If I can see that to learn about tolerance, my opponent is my best teacher...

Slander is a poison which kills charity, both in the slanderer and the one who listens.

St Bernard

ABSENCE OF CRITICISM

If I can be quick with sincere praise

but not so ready to criticize or blame...

I believe that justice is instinctive and innate, that the moral sense is as much a part of our constitution as that of feeling, seeing and hearing.

Thomas Jefferson

JUSTICE

If I can resist the overwhelming urge to have more than is necessary...

Two things profoundly impress me; the starry heavens above me and the moral law within me.

Immanuel Kant

LAWFULNESS

If I can direct my life along the straight path of the law...

Two works of mercy

set a man free;

forgive and you will be forgiven,

and give and you will receive.

St Augustine of Hippo

MERCY

If I can see that
Mercy and Justice

reflect the finest
qualities of
Heart and Mind...

The good man does not consider gold and jade to be precious treasures, but loyalty and good faith.

Confucius

LOYALTY

If I can see that the
real strength of a
family, team or
nation is our loyalty
to each other...

Respect man as a spiritual being in whom dwells the Divine Spirit.

Leo Tolstoy

RESPECT

Far better to do your own duty imperfectly than to do the duty of another perfectly.

Bhagavad Gita

DUTY

If I can make sure that I never let down a friend in need...

Give what you have to someone, it may be better than you dare think.

Henry Wadsworth Longfellow

SERVICE

If I can serve others by
helping them to discover
their true nature...

Temperance...which consists in not being transported by the passions, but in controlling them with coolness and moderation.

Plato

TEMPERANCE

If I can work on
minimising my desires
and living moderately...

Moderation is desirable in every affair.

Bahá'u'lláh

MODERATION

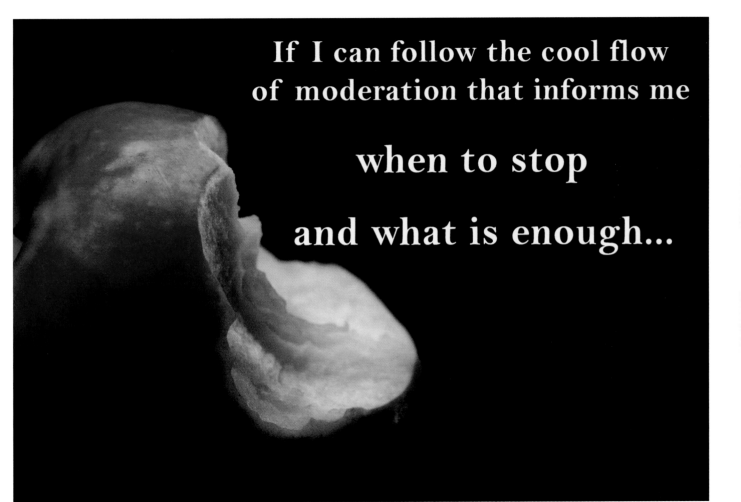

If I can follow the cool flow
of moderation that informs me

when to stop

and what is enough...

Not he who has little, but he who desires much is poor.

Seneca

ABSENCE OF GREED

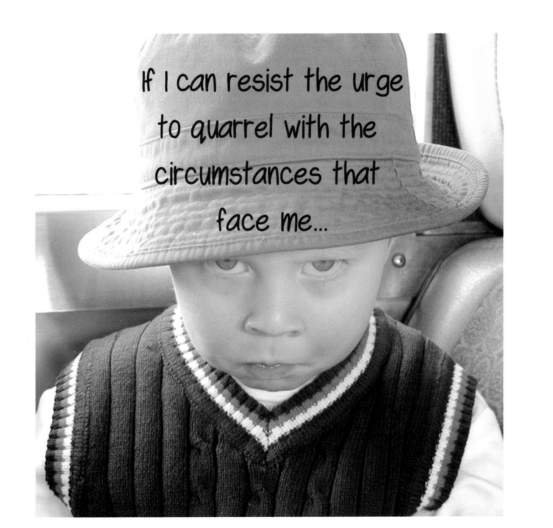

There is a courageous wisdom; there is also a false, reptile prudence, the result, not of caution, but of fear.

Edmund Burke

PRUDENCE

If I can see that to trust everyone is foolish, but to trust men of worth is prudent...

A state of harmony with nature, with all beings in the creation, itself leads to harmony with humanity. If we lose our relationship with nature, we inevitably lose our relationship with humanity.

Krishnamurti

HARMONY

To be meek, patient, tactful, modest, honourable, brave, is not to be either manly or womanly; it is to be human.

Jane Harrison

TACTFULNESS

If I can learn to make a point,

without making an enemy...

Remember this - there is a proper dignity and proportion to be observed in the performance of every act of life.

Marcus Aurelius

DIGNITY

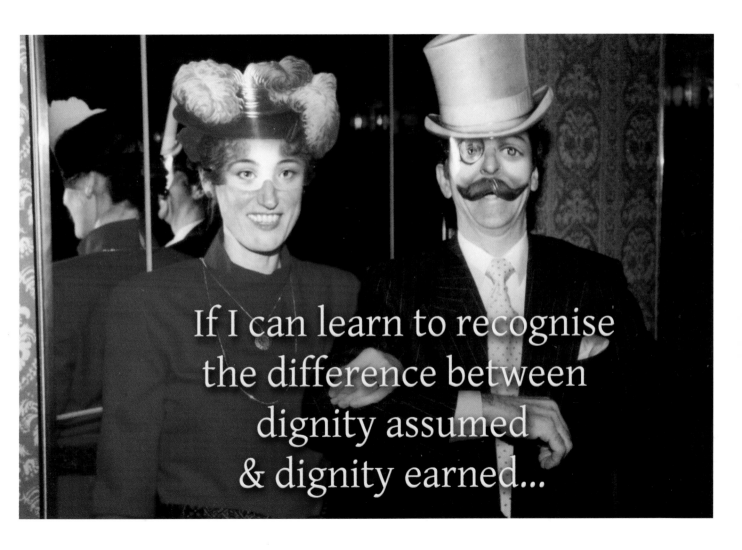

If I can learn to recognise
the difference between
dignity assumed
& dignity earned...

Remember the Truth,
Remember Its simplicity,
Remember It never changes,
Remember that It is eternal and
Remember that It is your own self.

Leon MacLaren

TRUTHFULNESS

If I can realise that to tell the truth is

Natural

and gives me

Freedom...

Trust the past to God's mercy, the present to God's love and the future to God's providence.

St Augustine of Hippo

TRUST

God prefers him who honours the poor, to him who worships the wealthy.

Instructions of Amenemope

HONOUR

If I can learn

to honour
the small

as well as the large...

Let your words correspond with your actions and your actions with your words.

Confucius

INTEGRITY

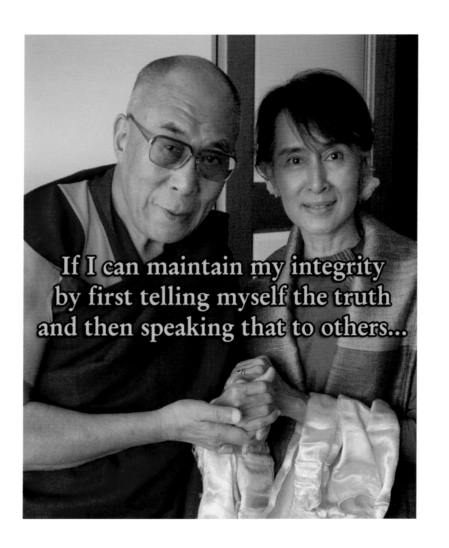

This above all,

To thine own self be true;

And it must follow as the night the day,

Thou canst not then be false to any man.

Shakespeare, Hamlet

RELIABILITY

Sincerity,
a deep, great, genuine sincerity
is the first characteristic
of all men who are in
anyway heroic.

Thomas Carlyle

SINCERITY

If I can see that sincerity
and competence are
a very powerful duo...

Faithful friends are a sturdy shelter; whoever finds one has found a treasure. Faithful friends are beyond price; no amount can balance their worth.

Ecclesiastes

FRIENDSHIP

What a piece of work is man.
How noble in reason.
How infinite in faculty.

Shakespeare

WISDOM

If I can look for and find,

a wise teacher...

To produce without possessing,
to work without expecting,
to enlarge without usurping,
to know
when you have had enough,
is to be rich.   Lao Tsu

DETACHMENT

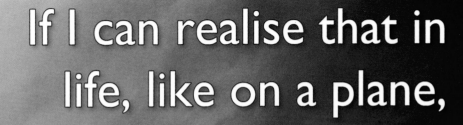

If I can realise that in
life, like on a plane,

I have to pay

for the excess baggage
of my attachments...

Each person has inside a basic decency and goodness. If he listens to it and acts on it, he is giving a great deal of what the world needs most.

Pablo Casals

DISCRIMINATION

If I can keep reminding myself
that the answer to the question,
'TO BE or NOT TO BE'
is

TO BE...

For I am fresh of spirit and resolved to meet all perils very constantly.

Shakespeare

CONSISTENCY

If I can avoid getting continually distracted and simply stick to the point...

The spirit of man loves purity,
but the mind disturbs it.
Let the mind be made clean
and his spirit will of itself
become pure.

Lao Tzu

PURITY OF MIND

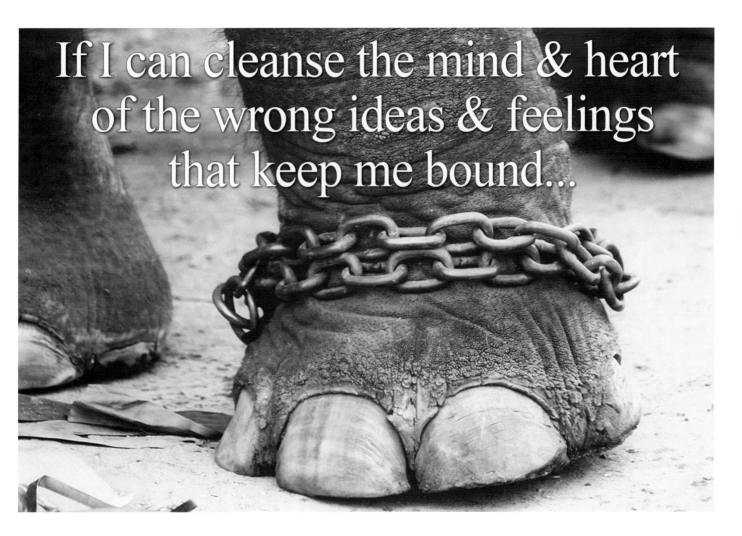

If I can cleanse the mind & heart
of the wrong ideas & feelings
that keep me bound...

The work of righteousness
shall be peace;
and the effect of righteousness-
quietness and assurance forever.

Isaiah 32:17

RIGHTEOUNESS

If I can be disciplined and transparent
so that there is no taint of corruption...

To meditate does not only mean to examine, observe, reflect, question, weigh; it also has a more profound meaning which is 'to become.'

Krishnamurti

MEDITATION

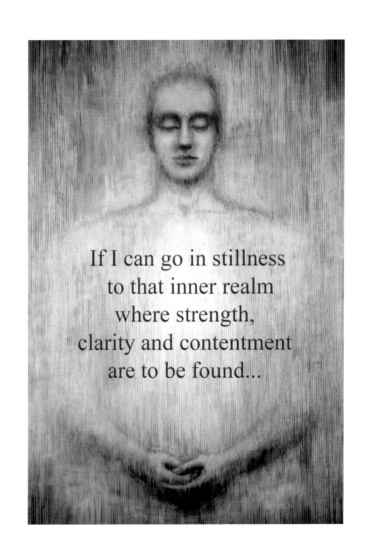

If I can go in stillness
to that inner realm
where strength,
clarity and contentment
are to be found...

Set no value on property,
seek no honours.
Avoid excess,
avoid restlessness.
Rejoice in the present.

Marsilio Ficino

BEING PRESENT

Make pain and pleasure,
loss and gain,
victory and defeat equal to you,
then turn yourself to battle,
and so you shall have no sin.

Krishna-Bhagavad Gita

EQUANIMITY

IF I CAN REMAIN CENTRED,

WITHOUT ATTACHMENT,

RETAINING BALANCE,

TOUCHING NOTHING...

When evil times prevail,
take care to preserve
the serenity of your heart.

Horace

SERENITY

If I can still my mind,

calm my emotions

and master my will...

In the attitude of silence
the soul finds the path
in a clearer light,
and what is elusive and deceptive
resolves itself into crystal clearness.

Mahatma Gandhi

STILLNESS

**If I can realise the value
of silence & stillness**

**which is so necessary
in our restless age...**

Possessions, outward success, publicity, luxury-to me these have always been contemptible.
I believe that a simple and unassuming manner of life is
best for everyone,
best for both body and mind.

Einstein

SIMPLICITY

If I can stay with the simple,
the HERE & NOW
and
avoid the complicated,
the THERE & THEN...

Creativity requires the courage to let go of certainties.

Eric Fromm

CREATIVITY

If I can

realise that

creativity is

a great gift

to be used

for the benefit

of all...

Concentration of the powers of the Spirit to discover unity in diversity is called consciousness.

Swami Vivekananda

CONSCIOUSNESS

If I can learn how to
consciously let go of
all attachment to the
results of my actions,
be they good or bad...

God made sense turn outward,
man therefore looks outward.
Now and again a daring soul
desiring immortality
looks back and finds himself.

Katha Upanishad

SPIRITUALITY

If I can accept that everything in creation
is born,
flourishes,
decays &
then dies...

You will never be an inwardly religious and devout person unless you pass over in silence the shortcomings of your fellow men, and diligently examine your own weaknesses.

Thomas à Kempis

DEVOTION

If I can apply myself
with single-minded
devotion

to the task in hand...

Nothing so cements and holds
together all the parts of a society
as faith or credit, which can never
be kept up unless men are under some
force or necessity of honestly paying
what they owe to one another.

Cicero

FAITH

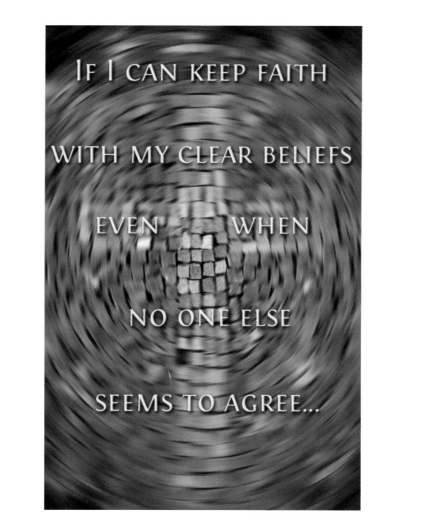

Hope is practised through the virtue of patience, which continues to do good even in the face of apparent failure, and through the virtue of humility, which accepts God's mystery and trusts him even at times of darkness.

Pope Benedict XVI

HOPE

If I can dare to dream,
knowing that I may
be disappointed,
but still let hope
reign supreme...

Peace is not something you must hope for in the future.
Rather it is a deepening of the present, and unless you look for it in the present you will never find it.

Thomas Merton

PEACE

If I can see that true peace
is to be found in the
present moment
...and nowhere else...

The universe will help us achieve our mission & vision, if it is good for all.

Hari Prasad Kanoria

UNITY

If I can see that all
the different waves
are made of the
same water...

Freedom is for Love.

It is given to man as a task

to be accomplished.

There is no freedom without truth.

Pope John Paul II

FREEDOM

Our task must be
to free ourselves
by widening our
circle of compassion
to embrace all living creatures
and the whole of nature
and its beauty.

Einstein

BEAUTY

If I can see the same beauty
in the rainbow's arch,
in a mother's tender care
and in the people I meet
every day...

That which is infinite
is alone happiness.
There is no happiness
in anything finite.

Chandogya Upanishad

HAPPINESS

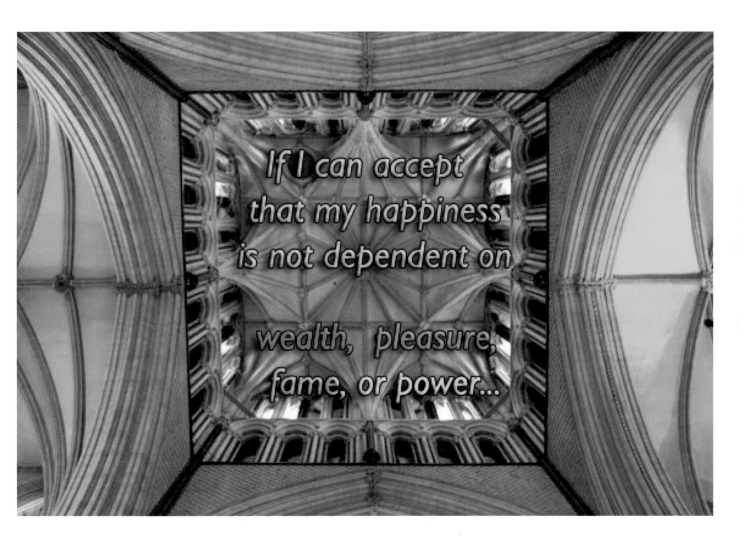

If I can accept
that my happiness
is not dependent on

wealth, pleasure,
fame, or power...

Peace to him who has finished the supreme journey under the guidance of the Truth and the Light.

Baha'a'llah

LIBERATION

THEN

I WILL BE AN

INSTRUMENT

FOR PEACE

IN THE

WORLD...

Acknowledgements

We would like to acknowledge both the talent and the generosity of the photographers and artists who have provided the images in this book. We have obtained some of the photos under the Creative Commons license and there are a small number where we were unable to identify the source. We have tried to establish attribution for all images used in this book and the related online app, www.ificanapp.com.
If we have missed any, we apologise and will add these in future revisions.

The photographers and artists who contributed to the images in this book are:

Blaq Annabiosis
Matteo Bagnoli
Vinoth Chandar
Orman Clark
Jeffery Courtney
Charles Hardaker
Patrik Jones
P J Jupp
Jeff Kubina
George Lubikowski
Martin Lubikowski
Ronald Nydegger
Paul Palmarozza

Alex E Proimos
D Sharon Pruitt
Chris Rees
Jerome Toole
Sherrie Thai
Trevor Waldron
Brian Wolfe
Brian Wright
Dirk Wuestenhagen
Richard Wythe
Wandering Angel
Fussy Onion

All the quotations used have been sourced from a variety of free access websites.